The
Harpooner

a Devotional Guide for Advent

for Laura

© 2013, Thomas McKenzie
www.ThomasMcKenzie.com
Thomas@ThomasMcKenzie.com
Nashville, Tennessee

Edited by Ella H. McKenzie

ALL RIGHTS RESERVED. This book contains material protected under International and Federal Copyright Laws and Treaties. Any unauthorized reprint or use of this material is prohibited. No part of this book may be reproduced or transmitted in any form or by any means, electronic or mechanical, including photocopying, recording, or by any information storage and retrieval system without express written permission from the author, except for the use of brief quotations for book review or educational purposes with citation.

Scripture quotations marked (NIV) are taken from the Holy Bible, New International Version®, NIV®. Copyright © 1973, 1978, 1984, 2011 by Biblica, Inc.™ Used by permission of Zondervan. All rights reserved worldwide. www.zondervan.com The "NIV" and "New International Version" are trademarks registered in the United States Patent and Trademark Office by Biblica, Inc.™

All Psalms, or portions of Psalms, are in the Public Domain, and come from the Book of Common Prayer, 1979, published by the Church Hymnal Corporation, New York. All sentences labeled "Prayer of the Day" are the Collects of the Day found in this same Book of Common Prayer, and are also in the Public Domain.

Cover Illustration: Queequeg and his Harpoon, from Moby Dick, Charles Scribner's Sons, New York, 1902, in the Public Domain.

Table of Contents

Title Page
Dedication and Copyright

Introduction ... The Harpooner	page 4
Dec. 1 ... We Begin at the End	page 8
Dec. 2 ... My Favorite Collect	page 10
Dec. 3 ... Pie Jesu	page 12
Dec. 4 ... The Two Seasons	page 15
Dec. 5 ... An Obstructed View	page 17
Dec. 6 ... The Coming Thief	page 20
Dec. 7 ... A Gift to the Poor	page 23
Dec. 8 ... The Word Came to John	page 26
Dec. 9 ... Familiar as the Moon	page 28
Dec. 10 ... Good Boys	page 30
Dec. 11 ... The Accuser	page 33
Dec. 12 ... Promises and Patience	page 36
Dec. 13 ... Re-Ordered	page 39
Dec. 14 ... The Advent Fast	page 41
Dec. 15 ... Blessed is She	page 43
Dec. 16 ... When Advent Fails	page 46
Dec. 17 ... Kingdom Come	page 49
Dec. 18 ... There is No Santa Claus	page 51
Dec. 19 ... No Room in the House	page 53
Dec. 20 ... The Sign of Jonah	page 56
Dec. 21 ... Can I Get an Amen?	page 58
Dec. 22 ... Blessed is He	page 61
Dec. 23 ... Steward and King	page 64
Dec. 24 ... Christmas Eve	page 67
Dec. 25 ... Emmanuel	page 70
About the Author	page 72

Introduction

The Harpooner

In his recent memoir, Eugene Peterson compares the life of a pastor to the role of a harpooner on a nineteenth-century whaling ship. A harpooner was the member of the crew whose task was to throw his harpoon at the whale when the ship was close enough. While the rest of the crew struggled against the wind and waves, the harpooner waited, conserving his strength for the perfect moment. Eugene Peterson says it this way:

> In Herman Melville's Moby Dick, there is a turbulent scene in which a whaleboat scuds across a frothing ocean in pursuit of the great white whale, Moby Dick. The sailors are laboring fiercely, every muscle taut, all attention and energy concentrated on the task. The cosmic conflict between good and evil is joined; chaotic sea and demonic sea monster versus the morally outraged man, Captain Ahab. In this boat, however, there is one man who does nothing. He doesn't hold an oar; he doesn't perspire; he doesn't shout. He is languid in the crash and the cursing. This man is the harpooner, quiet and poised, waiting. And then this sentence: "To insure the greatest efficiency in the dart, the harpooners of this world must start to their feet out of idleness, and not out of toil." ...
>
> History is a novel of spiritual conflict. The church is a whaleboat. In such a world, noise is inevitable, and immense energy is expended. But if there is no harpooner in the boat, there will be no proper finish to the chase. Or if the harpooner is exhausted, having abandoned his assignment and become an oarsman, he will not be ready and accurate when it is time to throw his javelin...
>
> Somehow it always seems more compelling to assume the work of the oarsman, laboring mightily in a moral cause, throwing our energy into a fray we know has immortal consequence. And it always seems more dramatic to take on the outrage of a Captain Ahab, obsessed with a vision of vengeance and retaliation, brooding over the ancient injury done by the Enemy.

There is, though, other important work to do. Someone must throw the dart. Some must be harpooners.

- Eugene Peterson, *The Pastor*, page 281-282.

I have one small disagreement with Eugene Peterson. While he sees this as a way of describing the life of a pastor, I see it as a metaphor for the best kind of Christian life.

We are called to live a life of waiting. Of course, there will be moments of strife, and we should be ready for them. But we must resist the voices that say we must be always fighting, always struggling. These voices tempt us to use all our strength in some righteous cause, throwing ourselves against the merciless storm of evil in the world. They lead us to believe that we will conquer our enemies, but the truth is that we will only destroy ourselves. Instead, we must learn the truth that God is the mighty warrior, he is the Victorious One. He is strong enough to conquer the darkness, I am not.

Life is not about doing great things for God. Most of life is simply about being present, waiting upon the Lord, and responding when we're called. This is what it means to be a harpooner.

Jesus was once asked, "What must we do to do the works God requires? (John 6:28, NIV)." That is the question that most religious people ask. We want to know what we're supposed to do in order to please God, we want to be acceptable to him. Many of us want a definite list of moral principles that they must obey. Others want to know exactly what doctrines we need to believe. Still others want to be sent into battle against the world and the devil. We want to "take a hill for Jesus," as I once heard an excited pastor declare.

But the Lord has something different in mind. "Jesus answered them, 'The work of God is this: to believe in the one he has sent' (John 6:29, NIV)." The work of God is to trust Jesus. Doing good deeds, believing the right things, and struggling against the temptations of this world are all important. But the one thing God is most interested in is that we simply rest in the love of his Son.

Resting is not laziness. We aren't called to lie stagnant, like a couch potato vegging out in front of daytime T.V. Quite the opposite. We're called to rest like a harpooner, strong and prepared to act. Jesus put it this way in Mark's Gospel:

> Be on guard! Be alert! You do not know when that time will come. It's like a man going away: He leaves his house and puts his servants in charge, each with their assigned task, and tells the one at the door to keep watch. Therefore keep watch because you do not know when the owner of the house will come back—whether in the evening, or at midnight, or when the rooster crows, or at dawn. If he comes suddenly, do not let him find you sleeping. What I say to you, I say to everyone: 'Watch!' (Mark 13:33-37, NIV)

Waiting on the Lord, being on guard until the time to act–this is the theme of Advent. But what does that look like? How do you "watch" in the real world? The purpose of this devotional guide is to help train your soul, to aid the Spirit's work of forming you into a harpooner.

Advent and Christmas

The word "Christmas" means more than one thing. It's the name of a shopping season, a stressful time of mall crawling and credit card maxing. Christmas is also a season of culture, concerts, and parties. Further, it's the name of a family holiday, a day set aside to be with those closest to you (or, at least those you're related to).

Historically, Christians haven't meant any of those things when we say "Christmas." Rather, we're speaking of a holy season dedicated to retelling the story of the Son of God becoming the Son of Man.

The festival of God's Incarnation, the Christ-Mass, was being celebrated in the Church by about 220 A.D. In the ancient world, fasting came before feasting. It was natural to the Early Church that a season of self-examination and repentance would lead up to the great Christmas festival. By the fourth-century A.D., the four Sundays preceding Christmas were set aside to prepare for the Coming of Christ. They called this the season of Advent.

The word "Advent" comes from the Latin world *adventus*, which means "coming." Members of the Church prepared for first coming of Christ, when he visited us as an infant in the manger. But they also made ready for the second coming of Christ. This normally meant entering a time of fasting, prayer, and special acts of devotion.

Today, large parts of the Church have forgotten Advent. We feast constantly, and rarely fast. We've confused shopping, parties, and concerts with waiting for Christ. Thankfully, many Christians are rediscovering the beauty of Advent. I hope this guidebook will help you prepare for the Lord in this season.

Using This Book

This book will guide you through Advent. The Season of Advent sometimes begins in the last days of November or the early days of December; but, to make this book more useful, we'll stick to the calendar month of December.

There's a short chapter for each day of the month. It's best to read one chapter a day. If you skip a day, don't feel the need to go back. Have some grace with yourself.

Each chapter begins with the Prayer of the Day, which comes from the Anglican Church. Start by praying that prayer, either silently or aloud. Next, read the scripture for the day. Spend a few moments in silence before you move on.

After the scripture reading is the homily. This is a personal reflection meant to help you know the Lord a bit better. Following the homily is a psalm, or part of a psalm, chosen to go along with the homily and scripture. The psalm is meant to be prayed, either silently or aloud. You may want to finish your time with the Lord's Prayer, or a short period of silence, or a time of personal prayer. Following this simple pattern of prayer, scripture, and listening is one way of opening yourself to the Holy Spirit.

Besides reading a chapter a day in this book, you may consider other Advent practices. These might include giving up something like alcohol, sugar, or Facebook. You could decide to spend more concentrated time with family and friends, or to spend an morning alone in nature, or to do some act of service for your church or your community. None of that is required, of course; but it might help you know Jesus more deeply. Better knowing the love of God in Jesus Christ is the best possible result of walking through the Advent season.

December First

The Prayer of the Day

Almighty God, give us grace to cast away the works of darkness, and put on the armor of light, now in the time of this mortal life in which your Son Jesus Christ came to visit us in great humility; that in the last day, when he shall come again in his glorious majesty to judge both the living and the dead, we may rise to the life immortal; through him who lives and reigns with you and the Holy Spirit, one God, now and for ever. Amen.

Scripture: 2 Peter 3:3-4, 8-10 (NIV)

Above all, you must understand that in the last days scoffers will come, scoffing and following their own evil desires. They will say, "Where is this 'coming' he promised? Ever since our ancestors died, everything goes on as it has since the beginning of creation."

But do not forget this one thing, dear friends: With the Lord a day is like a thousand years, and a thousand years are like a day. The Lord is not slow in keeping his promise, as some understand slowness. Instead he is patient with you, not wanting anyone to perish, but everyone to come to repentance. But the day of the Lord will come like a thief. The Heavens will disappear with a roar; the elements will be destroyed by fire, and the earth and everything done in it will be laid bare.

Homily: We Begin at the End

Sometimes, a movie drops you right into the middle of the action. The first scene opens on a critical moment of life or death. The bad guy is standing over the hero, the bomb is seconds away from exploding, and all hope is lost. Then, the camera cuts to an image of a boat on the water or a sports car driving through the mountains. Words appear at the bottom of the screen: "48 hours earlier." The story restarts, building up to that intense moment you've already seen.

Advent is like that. We don't start with a baby in a manger or a wise man on a camel. We start with fire. We begin at the End. Many years, the first Sunday in Advent is also the Sunday after Thanksgiving, a shock to the system after a few bloated days of turkey and football.

But that's the way Jesus promised to return. Not at a convenient time, not on a day we're ready for him. He's coming again like a thief, sneaking up on us when we're fat and sleepy.

Does the image of the sky ripped apart scare you? Does the idea of all your life being laid bare before the universe make you uncomfortable? Does the end of God's patience give you pause? If the answer is "yes," then you are in a good place. You might be ready for Advent.

Advent is meant to be uncomfortable. At the same time, it's deeply comforting. The return of Christ means that God is in charge of the universe. The story of our collective lives has a purpose. Everything, and everyone, means something in the end.

Psalm 111

Hallelujah!
> I will give thanks to the Lord with my whole heart,
>> in the assembly of the upright, in the congregation.

Great are the deeds of the Lord!
> they are studied by all who delight in them.

His work is full of majesty and splendor,
> and his righteousness endures for ever.

He makes his marvelous works to be remembered;
> the Lord is gracious and full of compassion.

He gives food to those who fear him;
> he is ever mindful of his covenant.

He has shown his people the power of his works
> in giving them the lands of the nations.

The works of his hands are faithfulness and justice;
> all his commandments are sure.

They stand fast for ever and ever,
> because they are done in truth and equity.

He sent redemption to his people; he commanded his
> covenant for ever; holy and awesome is his Name.

The fear of the Lord is the beginning of wisdom;
> those who act accordingly have a good understanding;
> his praise endures for ever.

December Second

The Prayer of the Day

Almighty God, give us grace to cast away the works of darkness, and put on the armor of light, now in the time of this mortal life in which your Son Jesus Christ came to visit us in great humility; that in the last day, when he shall come again in his glorious majesty to judge both the living and the dead, we may rise to the life immortal; through him who lives and reigns with you and the Holy Spirit, one God, now and for ever. Amen.

Scripture: Romans 13:11-14 (NIV)

And do this, understanding the present time: The hour has already come for you to wake up from your slumber, because our salvation is nearer now than when we first believed. The night is nearly over; the day is almost here. So let us put aside the deeds of darkness and put on the armor of light. Let us behave decently, as in the daytime, not in carousing and drunkenness, not in sexual immorality and debauchery, not in dissension and jealousy. Rather, clothe yourselves with the Lord Jesus Christ, and do not think about how to gratify the desires of the flesh.

Homily: My Favorite Collect

During worship in the first week of Advent, Anglican congregations around the world will pray together a "collect" from the great theologian Thomas Cranmer. These words prayerfully frame the meaning of the Advent season. In Cranmer's original version, the prayer goes like this:

> Almighty God, give us grace that we may cast away the works of darkness, and put upon us the armour of light, now in the time of this mortal life, in which thy Son Jesus Christ came to visit us in great humility; that in the last day, when he shall come again in his glorious Majesty, to judge both the quick and the dead, we may rise to the life immortal; through him who liveth and reigneth with thee and the Holy Ghost, now and ever. Amen.

During Advent, the Church prepares for both the First Coming of Christ (the Incarnation) and for the Second Coming (the End of the

Age). You see both of these in this prayer. "This mortal life in which Christ came to visit us in great humility" is his Incarnation. "The last day, when he shall come again" is his second coming.

The prayer comes from the Bible verse above, Romans 13:12, weaving together this passage with the meaning of the season. We ask God for a twofold blessing. First, we ask for grace to leave aside our sinful actions. With God's help we will repent, abandoning our destructive paths. Second, by grace we hope to put on the whole armor of God (Ephesians 6:10, etc.). We can step boldly forward, trusting in Christ.

Both the First and Second Coming are about the true light coming into the world. So the prayer uses the imagery of light and darkness, as well as other poetic phrases like "this mortal life" vs "the life immortal." It's a poetic prayer, a biblical prayer. It lifts us up to God during this holy season. In the midst of all the busyness of life, I commend it to your use, both today and in the season to come.

Psalm 2:1-8, 12

Why are the nations in an uproar?
>Why do the peoples mutter empty threats?

Why do the kings of the earth rise up in revolt,
>and the princes plot together,
>against the Lord and against his Anointed?

"Let us break their yoke," they say;
>"let us cast off their bonds from us."

He whose throne is in Heaven is laughing;
>the Lord has them in derision.

Then he speaks to them in his wrath,
>and his rage fills them with terror.

"I myself have set my king
>upon my holy hill of Zion."

Let me announce the decree of the Lord:
>he said to me, "You are my Son; this day have I begotten you.

Ask of me, and I will give you the nations for your inheritance
>and the ends of the earth for your possession…

Happy are they all
>who take refuge in him!

December Third

The Prayer of the Day

Almighty God, give us grace to cast away the works of darkness, and put on the armor of light, now in the time of this mortal life in which your Son Jesus Christ came to visit us in great humility; that in the last day, when he shall come again in his glorious majesty to judge both the living and the dead, we may rise to the life immortal; through him who lives and reigns with you and the Holy Spirit, one God, now and for ever. Amen.

Scripture: 2 Timothy 3:1-5 (NIV)

But mark this: There will be terrible times in the last days. People will be lovers of themselves, lovers of money, boastful, proud, abusive, disobedient to their parents, ungrateful, unholy, without love, unforgiving, slanderous, without self-control, brutal, not lovers of the good, treacherous, rash, conceited, lovers of pleasure rather than lovers of God—having a form of godliness but denying its power. Have nothing to do with such people.

Homily: *Pie Jesu*

Last year, my wife and I attended the Winter Concert at our daughter's school. It's a secular school, so I was not offended that there were no Christmas songs. I was, however, struck by something. One of the songs they performed was a version of *Pie Jesu*. As a reminder, *Pie Jesu* is part of the Latin Requiem Mass. It is typically sung as a prayer for the dead. While it can be translated in a number of ways, the words essentially mean "kind Lord Jesus, grant them rest."

There are a number of girls in the choir, including my daughter, who are studying Latin. So, at least some people at the concert knew what the words meant. I am assuming, though, that this song was not selected because of its meaning. In fact, it seemed strangely out of context. I would venture to say they would not have sung it in English—this sad song, this plea for the dead. So, why was it selected? I assume because it's a lovely setting and pleasing to listen to.

I enjoyed listening to the song. However, I felt somewhat unsettled. Here is a prayer for the dead in Christ, many of whom are friends of mine, being sung simply for the pleasure of the audience. It brought to mind Paul's phrase "having a form of godliness but denying its power" (2 Timothy 3:4, NIV).

December is a month filled with such unsettling moments. We will hear praises to Christ sung in the mall and on secular radio. We will see images of Christ displayed on napkins and pick-up trucks. We will see references to the Mass of Christ (Christmas) constantly used in advertising. Most of us will see or hear this, but not register what is happening. Our culture is taking one of the most blessed and beautiful events in cosmic history, the Incarnation of the Son of God, and using it for decoration. They are using the Lord of Glory to sell cars.

Of course, I could ignore all of this. I could say that it's not a big deal. As an alternative, I could use this as a reason to be offended. I could be that person who says "Merry CHRISTMAS" as an angry retort to someone else's "Happy Holidays." But then, wouldn't I be one of those "without love" whom Paul warns about in our scripture passage?

Rather than being either of those, I am asking God for the grace to respond differently. When I see the name of Christ used in secular space this season, I want to do two things. First, I want to thank God that his name is going out to people who might otherwise not hear it. What a strange wonder it would be if some non-Christian were to truly listen to *Silent Night* in Target and be transformed by the Holy Spirit! Second, I want to register in my heart the beauty of Jesus. When I hear *Hark the Herald* I want to have the grace to rejoice with the Angels, even if I am rejoicing in my dentist's office.

I'm glad those girls sang *Pie Jesu*. Most of them probably weren't intentionally praying those words, but I was. May we all have such moments this Advent season.

Psalm 11

In the Lord have I taken refuge;
>   how then can you say to me,
>   "Fly away like a bird to the hilltop;
For see how the wicked bend the bow
>   and fit their arrows to the string,
>   to shoot from ambush at the true of heart.
When the foundations are being destroyed,
>   what can the righteous do?"
The Lord is in his holy temple;
>   the Lord's throne is in Heaven.
His eyes behold the inhabited world;
>   his piercing eye weighs our worth.
The Lord weighs the righteous as well as the wicked,
>   but those who delight in violence he abhors.
Upon the wicked he shall rain coals of fire and burning sulphur;
>   a scorching wind shall be their lot.
For the Lord is righteous;
>   he delights in righteous deeds;
>   and the just shall see his face.

December Fourth

The Prayer of the Day

Almighty God, give us grace to cast away the works of darkness, and put on the armor of light, now in the time of this mortal life in which your Son Jesus Christ came to visit us in great humility; that in the last day, when he shall come again in his glorious majesty to judge both the living and the dead, we may rise to the life immortal; through him who lives and reigns with you and the Holy Spirit, one God, now and for ever. Amen.

Scripture: John 14:23-27 (NIV)

Jesus replied, "Anyone who loves me will obey my teaching. My Father will love them, and we will come to them and make our home with them. Anyone who does not love me will not obey my teaching. These words you hear are not my own; they belong to the Father who sent me. All this I have spoken while still with you. But the Advocate, the Holy Spirit, whom the Father will send in my name, will teach you all things and will remind you of everything I have said to you. Peace I leave with you; my peace I give you. I do not give to you as the world gives. Do not let your hearts be troubled and do not be afraid."

Homily: The Two Seasons

We are living in two seasons at once, whether we like it or not. Both seasons are about expectation. Both have music and candles and sparkling lights. Both seasons are building up to December 25th. One is the Holy Season of Advent, the other is the Christmas Shopping Season.

These two seasons happen at the same time, but they are not the same. The Advent Season is a time of expectation, of watching for Christ. The Christmas Shopping Season is a time of expectation, too. You are expected to give the right gifts, and you expect to get the right gifts in return.

The Christmas Shopping Season is an anxious place. Everything about it depends on you. You have to buy the presents. You have to throw a great party. You have to send cards to the right people. You have to cook the food and hang the lights. You have to pay the bills. You have to make sure not to forget anyone. If you mess up, people will get their feelings hurt. Will you have enough time, enough energy, enough money?

Advent, on the other hand, is a peaceful place because none of it depends on you. Christ came, and you can't change that. Christ is coming again, no matter what you do or don't do. You can choose to participate by praying for his grace, and by keeping your eyes open. But whether you stay alert or not, he's likely to interrupt your life.

We live simultaneously in Advent and the Christmas Shopping Season. By God's grace, we can focus on one more than another. Through prayer and scripture reading, we can set aside a little anxiety and ask for a little more peace. We can choose to turn our attention to the coming Christ, rather than the coming crisis. Perhaps, a little at a time, we may find ourselves living more fully in the Holy Season.

Psalm 12

Help me, Lord, for there is no godly one left;
> the faithful have vanished from among us.

Everyone speaks falsely with his neighbor;
> with a smooth tongue they speak from a double heart.

Oh, that the Lord would cut off all smooth tongues,
> and close the lips that utter proud boasts!

Those who say, "With our tongue will we prevail;
> our lips are our own; who is lord over us?"

"Because the needy are oppressed, and the poor cry out in misery,
> I will rise up," says the Lord,
> "and give them the help they long for."

The words of the Lord are pure words,
> like silver refined from ore
> and purified seven times in the fire.

O Lord, watch over us
> and save us from this generation for ever.

The wicked prowl on every side,
> and that which is worthless is highly prized by everyone.

December Fifth

The Prayer of the Day

Almighty God, give us grace to cast away the works of darkness, and put on the armor of light, now in the time of this mortal life in which your Son Jesus Christ came to visit us in great humility; that in the last day, when he shall come again in his glorious majesty to judge both the living and the dead, we may rise to the life immortal; through him who lives and reigns with you and the Holy Spirit, one God, now and for ever. Amen.

Scripture: John 14:8-14 (NIV)

Philip said, "Lord, show us the Father and that will be enough for us." Jesus answered: "Don't you know me, Philip, even after I have been among you such a long time? Anyone who has seen me has seen the Father. How can you say, 'Show us the Father'? Don't you believe that I am in the Father, and that the Father is in me? The words I say to you I do not speak on my own authority. Rather, it is the Father, living in me, who is doing his work. Believe me when I say that I am in the Father and the Father is in me; or at least believe on the evidence of the works themselves. Very truly I tell you, whoever believes in me will do the works I have been doing, and they will do even greater things than these, because I am going to the Father. And I will do whatever you ask in my name, so that the Father may be glorified in the Son. You may ask me for anything in my name, and I will do it."

Homily: An Obstructed View

Each Advent, I go to Nashville's historic Ryman Auditorium to see Andrew Peterson's "Behold the Lamb of God" show. I go because I love the music, but I also love the community. Andrew is a friend of mine, as are many of those who play with him. I look on stage and see people I know and love, and I run into many friends in the audience.

One year, I bought my tickets just days before the event. The ticketing website gave me its "best available seats," warning me that I would have an "obstructed view." Given that I could have these seats or none, I took them.

"Obstructed view" is a mild way of saying what we had. My wife and I were on the floor level, near the back of the room, as far to stage right as you could get. From where I sat, I could see only the front portion of the stage, and even half of that was blocked by a huge stack of speakers. I got to see Andrew Peterson and Andrew Osenga, which was nice, but I couldn't see anyone else. I could hear Andy and Jill, Ben and Randy, but see them? Not a chance.

The guy behind me was angrily telling his girlfriend how they "might as well have stayed home" and the "first thing I'm going to do tomorrow morning is call the ticket office." I, on the other hand, sat there beaming, crying, and singing along. I was sitting with my beloved wife, hearing great music, "seeing" good friends move in the gifts God has given them, and having a great time. Most importantly, I was hearing the grand story of the Gospel. No, I couldn't see everything. But I could hear, and what I heard, I loved.

Sometimes I have an obstructed view of God. I can't see him or what he's doing. Or I think I know what he's up to, and then something knocks me for a loop. I sometimes think I have things figured out, but then I am rudely awakened to the reality that I only see a small part of the stage, a fraction of the total picture. I don't have all the information, and neither does anyone else.

I can't always see God moving. I don't always experience him. But I can always listen to his voice. I can hear him in his Scriptures. Things may not look so great from where I'm sitting, but there is always Truth available to me. If I can put aside my indignation and anger for a minute, maybe I will hear something from the Lord.

Having an obstructed view of Christ doesn't mean he isn't there. Andy and Jill were on that stage, even though I did not see them. Likewise, God is in the midst of my little life, whether I happen to be staring at him in the face or straining my neck to catch a glimpse of his shoe.

Psalm 18:1-10

I love you, O Lord my strength,
> O Lord my stronghold, my crag, and my haven.

My God, my rock in whom I put my trust,
> my shield, the horn of my salvation,
> and my refuge; you are worthy of praise.

I will call upon the Lord,
> and so shall I be saved from my enemies.

The breakers of death rolled over me,
> and the torrents of oblivion made me afraid.

The cords of hell entangled me,
> and the snares of death were set for me.

I called upon the Lord in my distress
> and cried out to my God for help.

He heard my voice from his Heavenly dwelling;
> my cry of anguish came to his ears.

The earth reeled and rocked;
> the roots of the mountains shook;
> they reeled because of his anger.

Smoke rose from his nostrils
> and a consuming fire out of his mouth;
> hot burning coals blazed forth from him.

He parted the Heavens and came down
> with a storm cloud under his feet.

December Sixth

The Prayer of the Day

Almighty God, give us grace to cast away the works of darkness, and put on the armor of light, now in the time of this mortal life in which your Son Jesus Christ came to visit us in great humility; that in the last day, when he shall come again in his glorious majesty to judge both the living and the dead, we may rise to the life immortal; through him who lives and reigns with you and the Holy Spirit, one God, now and for ever. Amen.

Scripture: Matthew 24:36-44 (NIV)

But about that day or hour no one knows, not even the angels in Heaven, nor the Son, but only the Father. As it was in the days of Noah, so it will be at the coming of the Son of Man. For in the days before the flood, people were eating and drinking, marrying and giving in marriage, up to the day Noah entered the ark; and they knew nothing about what would happen until the flood came and took them all away. That is how it will be at the coming of the Son of Man. Two men will be in the field; one will be taken and the other left. Two women will be grinding with a hand mill; one will be taken and the other left.

Therefore keep watch, because you do not know on what day your Lord will come. But understand this: If the owner of the house had known at what time of night the thief was coming, he would have kept watch and would not have let his house be broken into. So you also must be ready, because the Son of Man will come at an hour when you do not expect him.

Homily: The Coming Thief

At one o'clock in the morning, I was downstairs in our den. I had twisted the television set around so I could get behind it. With a flashlight in one hand and a pen in the other, I was recording the TV's serial number. This seemed like a good idea at the time.

I live in a neighborhood that's usually pretty quiet, but there had been a number of burglaries recently. Two families in our church had had their houses broken into and their valuables stolen. Our friends who live four doors down were robbed. The thieves hit in the morning, just after our friends had left for work. They smashed in the back door and grabbed the electronics and jewelry.

As a husband and father of two girls, I am overly aware of the threat of home invasion. We have an alarm system, which we arm at night or whenever we leave the house. We have a dog. We have a fenced-in backyard that I keep chained and locked. We are careful.

But as careful as we are, I know that if a thief really wants to get in, he will. I sometimes have the sick feeling that such a crime is inevitable. I'm afraid that, one of these days, I'm going to come home to a burglarized house. Preparation is important, but ultimately, I am not in control. There is nothing I can do to guarantee our security.

In the scripture passage above, Jesus says that if the homeowner had known when the thief was coming, he could have stopped him. If my friend down the street had known what time the burglars were coming, I guarantee there would have been a shotgun waiting for them!

Jesus compares himself to that criminal. We don't know when to expect Christ. Advent is a time of preparation, and it's a time to accept the inevitable. Yes, we can prepare our hearts for Christ. But we don't control him. No matter what we do, or don't do, Christ is going to show up. He's going to come into our lives whether we ask him to or not. Of course, he doesn't come to steal! He comes to bring us life (John 10:10).

Though I know Jesus is good, he still scares me. I'd rather keep God at church, or in my prayer time, or in the Bible. He feels safe there. But he won't stay locked up in religion. He could invade my real life at any time. So I keep on the look out today, wondering when he might come.

Psalm 16:5-11

O Lord, you are my portion and my cup;
    it is you who uphold my lot.
My boundaries enclose a pleasant land;
    indeed, I have a goodly heritage.
I will bless the Lord who gives me counsel;
    my heart teaches me, night after night.
I have set the Lord always before me;
    because he is at my right hand I shall not fall.
My heart, therefore, is glad, and my spirit rejoices;
    my body also shall rest in hope.
For you will not abandon me to the grave,
    nor let your holy one see the Pit.
You will show me the path of life;
    in your presence there is fullness of joy,
        and in your right hand are pleasures for evermore.

December Seventh

The Prayer of the Day

Almighty God, give us grace to cast away the works of darkness, and put on the armor of light, now in the time of this mortal life in which your Son Jesus Christ came to visit us in great humility; that in the last day, when he shall come again in his glorious majesty to judge both the living and the dead, we may rise to the life immortal; through him who lives and reigns with you and the Holy Spirit, one God, now and for ever. Amen.

Scripture: Matthew 25:31-46 (NIV)

When the Son of Man comes in his glory, and all the angels with him, he will sit on his glorious throne. All the nations will be gathered before him, and he will separate the people one from another as a shepherd separates the sheep from the goats. He will put the sheep on his right and the goats on his left.

Then the King will say to those on his right, "Come, you who are blessed by my Father; take your inheritance, the kingdom prepared for you since the creation of the world. For I was hungry and you gave me something to eat, I was thirsty and you gave me something to drink, I was a stranger and you invited me in, I needed clothes and you clothed me, I was sick and you looked after me, I was in prison and you came to visit me."

Then the righteous will answer him, "Lord, when did we see you hungry and feed you, or thirsty and give you something to drink? When did we see you a stranger and invite you in, or needing clothes and clothe you? When did we see you sick or in prison and go to visit you?" The King will reply, "Truly I tell you, whatever you did for one of the least of these brothers and sisters of mine, you did for me."

Then he will say to those on his left, "Depart from me, you who are cursed, into the eternal fire prepared for the devil and his angels. For I was hungry and you gave me nothing to eat, I was thirsty and you gave me nothing to drink, I was a stranger and you did not invite me in, I needed clothes and you did not clothe me, I was sick and in prison and you did not look after me." They also will answer, "Lord, when did we see you hungry or thirsty or a stranger or needing clothes or sick or in prison, and did not help you?"

He will reply, "Truly I tell you, whatever you did not do for one of the least of these, you did not do for me." Then they will go away to eternal punishment, but the righteous to eternal life.

Homily: A Gift to the Poor

A few years ago, I took my girls to see Disney's animated film *A Christmas Carol*. Perhaps because Disney makes amusement park rides, part of the 3-D movie felt like being on a roller coaster. Speeding through the streets of Victorian England was pretty fun.

That wasn't what impressed me about the film, though. What really stood out was how devoted the script was to Charles Dickens's original novella. Because most of the film was taken word-for-word from Dickens, the point of that original story came through loud and clear–Christians are supposed to care for the poor. That's the point Dickens was making, and the movie pulled no punches. While I would argue that *A Christmas Carol* suffers from a hefty dose of works-based salvation, it certainly made an impression on my kids and me.

Advent is a season in which the Church looks ahead to the great Day of Judgment. On that Day, you and I will not be saved or damned because of how we treat the poor. Salvation is in Christ alone, by grace alone, through faith alone. But the Lord will also judge our works, including the way we treat the most vulnerable people. We will answer for our actions, or inactions.

In this season, it's important to spend some of our time, energy, and money on those who are less fortunate. Hopefully, there is a way to do that through your church. Another way that I recommend is through World Vision's Christmas Catalog. This catalog, available online, allows you to select gifts that will be given to the poor in the name of another person. So, instead of buying a sweater for your sister, you could give a goat to a family in Africa. Instead of buying mugs for your co-workers, you could provide a month of education to an orphan, or a fish pond for a village, or clothing for the homeless. World Vision will send your recipients a card, telling them about the gift given in their name. You can visit the Christmas Catalog by going to www.WorldVision.org.

Gift-giving is part of the tradition of Christmas. Some of the gifts we give this year could be a blessing to both the recipient and to a person in need. I especially think of those people who don't really need anything else, the man or woman "who has it all." Maybe this would be a good time of the year to feed the hungry and clothe the naked in their name, and in the Name of Jesus.

Psalm 117

Praise the Lord, all you nations;
>   laud him, all you peoples.
For his loving-kindness toward us is great,
>   and the faithfulness of the Lord endures for ever.
>   Hallelujah!

December Eighth

The Prayer of the Day

Merciful God, who sent your messengers the prophets to preach repentance and prepare the way for our salvation: Give us grace to heed their warnings and forsake our sins, that we may greet with joy the coming of Jesus Christ our Redeemer; who lives and reigns with you and the Holy Spirit, one God, now and for ever. Amen.

Scripture: Luke 3:1-3 (NIV)

In the fifteenth year of the reign of Tiberius Caesar—when Pontius Pilate was governor of Judea, Herod tetrarch of Galilee, his brother Philip tetrarch of Iturea and Traconitis, and Lysanias tetrarch of Abilene—during the high-priesthood of Annas and Caiaphas, the word of God came to John son of Zechariah in the wilderness. He went into all the country around the Jordan, preaching a baptism of repentance for the forgiveness of sins.

Homily: The Word of God Came to John

When I was in high school, our English teacher taught us about "The Great Chain of Being." This was a medieval world-view, a theory of the universe. God was at the top of the universe, the top of the Chain. Just below God and his angels was the Pope or the King, then the lords and bishops, then the knights and priests, then the serfs, then the underclasses, the Jews, and the Muslims. The Great Chain justified the "Divine Right of Kings," the domination of the lower classes by the upper classes.

This idea, that God or the gods are the top of a universal hierarchy, can be found in cultures all over the world and throughout history. The Great Chain was even part of the Roman Empire. Caesar was considered a god, and the Empire's ultimate connection with the Divine. The Jewish people had a similar belief, but in their case God was thought to reside in the Temple at Jerusalem. The High Priest, who entered the Most Holy Place once a year, was closer to God than any other man.

This is why the scripture reading above is so surprising. God has sent his Message to the world. The Message sees Caesar in Rome, but doesn't go to him. It sees all the rulers of Israel—Pilate, Herod,

Philip, and Lysanias—but it doesn't stop for them. It sees the High Priests in Jerusalem, but doesn't rest on them. It goes straight down the Great Chain of Being, all the way to the bottom, to a wild man in the desert.

God didn't choose to reveal himself to the great and mighty. Instead, he came to the lowly and the marginalized. This is not unusual for God; in fact, it is his normal pattern. There is no Great Chain of Being, no humans born to dominate others in God's name. God does not need religious hierarchy or political power. Rather, he is looking for people who are looking for him.

There is a lesson here: do not discount the lowly. The little old lady at church may know the Word of God far better than the pastor. The homeless man may have more wisdom than the college professor. The waitress at Waffle House may have a divine message for you. Look to the marginal, the very young, and the very old. Pay attention to the poor and the prisoner. Don't disregard them.

Don't disregard yourself, either. You may not be a biblical scholar, you may not have been a Christian for very long. That doesn't mean God can't reveal himself to you. He can, and he will.

Psalm 149

Hallelujah!
Sing to the Lord a new song;
    sing his praise in the congregation of the faithful.
Let Israel rejoice in his Maker;
    let the children of Zion be joyful in their King.
Let them praise his Name in the dance;
    let them sing praise to him with timbrel and harp.
For the Lord takes pleasure in his people
    and adorns the poor with victory.
Let the faithful rejoice in triumph;
    let them be joyful on their beds.
Let the praises of God be in their throat
    and a two-edged sword in their hand;
To wreak vengeance on the nations
    and punishment on the peoples;
To bind their kings in chains
    and their nobles with links of iron;
To inflict on them the judgment decreed;
    this is glory for all his faithful people. Hallelujah!

December Ninth

The Prayer of the Day

Merciful God, who sent your messengers the prophets to preach repentance and prepare the way for our salvation: Give us grace to heed their warnings and forsake our sins, that we may greet with joy the coming of Jesus Christ our Redeemer; who lives and reigns with you and the Holy Spirit, one God, now and for ever. Amen.

Scripture: Genesis 1:1-3, 14-18 (NIV)

In the beginning God created the Heavens and the earth. Now the earth was formless and empty, darkness was over the surface of the deep, and the Spirit of God was hovering over the waters. And God said, "Let there be light," and there was light. God saw that the light was good, and he separated the light from the darkness. God called the light "day," and the darkness he called "night."...

And God said, "Let there be lights in the vault of the sky to separate the day from the night, and let them serve as signs to mark sacred times, and days and years, and let them be lights in the vault of the sky to give light on the earth." And it was so. God made two great lights—the greater light to govern the day and the lesser light to govern the night. He also made the stars. God set them in the vault of the sky to give light on the earth, to govern the day and the night, and to separate light from darkness. And God saw that it was good.

Homily: Familiar as the Moon

Left His seamless robe behind
   Woke up in a stable and cried
Lived and died and rose again
   Savior for a guilty land
It's a story like a children's tune
   It's grown familiar as the moon
              --*There's Only One, written by Randall Goodgame*

It was a clear, unseasonably warm November night. I was driving up Franklin Road with the top down. The moon, high and bright, seemed to chase me over the hilltops. My car stereo was cranked up as I listened to Caedmon's Call perform *There's Only One*.

That moon—the one the band sang about, the one that chased me—is as ancient as anything I know. But the One who crafted it and set it spinning is more ancient still. His story is the first story. In a sense, it's the only story. All our stories, even the story of the moon, will culminate in a great End. That End will be Christ's Second Advent.

As far as I can tell, the Church has celebrated Advent for 1633 years. Surely, we have told the story of Christ's Visitation for longer, since the earliest days of the Church. But, by about 380 A.D., the Latin-speaking Church had begun to observe this time of preparation before the Christmas Festival.

Consider that for a moment—1633 years. More than eighty generations of Christians telling again and again the story of the Second Coming of Christ. When you've been waiting for something for a long time, it can be easy to forget what you are waiting for, or that you are waiting at all. When you've been waiting for someone to come back for 380 years? 2000 years? It may be that you need to set aside some time to remind yourself.

The story we tell every Advent is an old one. It is familiar, like a children's tune, familiar like the moon. But it must be told again. We share the story of Advent every year at this time. We share it so we can remember whom we are waiting for. We share it to remind one another to wait with hope. We share it because it's worth sharing, worth repeating, and worth telling. As familiar as the story is, it's still true. It's still beautiful. And one day, one of these Advents will be the last one.

Psalm 15

Lord, who may dwell in your tabernacle?
    who may abide upon your holy hill?
Whoever leads a blameless life and does what is right,
    who speaks the truth from his heart.
There is no guile upon his tongue; he does no evil to his friend;
    he does not heap contempt upon his neighbor.
In his sight the wicked is rejected,
    but he honors those who fear the Lord.
He has sworn to do no wrong
    and does not take back his word.
He does not give his money in hope of gain,
    nor does he take a bribe against the innocent.
Whoever does these things shall never be overthrown.

December Tenth

The Prayer of the Day

Merciful God, who sent your messengers the prophets to preach repentance and prepare the way for our salvation: Give us grace to heed their warnings and forsake our sins, that we may greet with joy the coming of Jesus Christ our Redeemer; who lives and reigns with you and the Holy Spirit, one God, now and for ever. Amen.

Scripture: Luke 12:35-37 (NIV)

Be dressed ready for service and keep your lamps burning, like servants waiting for their master to return from a wedding banquet, so that when he comes and knocks they can immediately open the door for him. It will be good for those servants whose master finds them watching when he comes. Truly I tell you, he will dress himself to serve, will have them recline at the table and will come and wait on them.

Homily: Good Boys

Who is the coolest Star Wars character? I'm sure you know the answer. I imagine one could argue it's Lando Calrissian (because he's played by Billy Dee Williams) or Boba Fett (because he's so mysterious, and owns a rocket backpack). But the obvious answer is Han Solo. The baddest good guy, or goodest bad guy, of the galaxy. The scoundrel, the pirate, the outlaw who ultimately wins the heart of a princess.

When I was a child, my favorite Star Wars character was Luke Skywalker. That's embarrassing to admit, but it's true. Why Luke, and not Han? Because Luke was a good boy. I wanted to be a good boy. I was the first born, the mature one, the moral one who didn't give mom and dad any trouble. Luke was the incarnation of good-boy-ness.

I wanted to be good, moral, and right. I grew up in a moralistic religion. Obeying the rules was important. It's no wonder that I wanted to be a priest. The pastorate is filled with grown-up good boys and girls.

A couple of years ago, I was present at an ordination during Advent. Yet another good person was becoming a pastor. But I was surprised, and delighted, by the Gospel reading that had been chosen. It was Luke 12:35-37, which you read above.

Do you see what happened in that text? It's easy to miss if you read it quickly. Jesus is telling us to be ready for his coming. He is the master, we are the slaves. We don't know when he will arrive. What happens when the master comes? He knocks on the door and finds the servants alert. Then the Master girds himself and serves the servants. The slaves recline at the table while the Lord waits on them. Jesus doesn't serve the slaves because they are good. He serves them because he came as a servant.

Jesus is not looking for good boys that he can launch on a dark world. Neither God nor the world need good boys. They don't need Luke Skywalkers. They don't need Han Solos, either. What the world and the Church need are sinners who will allow the Lord Jesus Christ to serve them. God is looking for the broken, not the perfect.

I am not good enough to be a priest. None of us are good enough to be Christians, the children of God, members of the New Covenant community. Rather, we are mere slaves who one day opened the door to find the Son of God standing there. He came to us. He served us from the Manger, to the Cross, to the Empty Tomb. In his Ascension, his sending of his Spirit, and in his promise to Return, he serves us still.

The best I can hope to be is a sinner who, served by Christ and graced by the Spirit, might occasionally find the strength to serve others in Jesus' Name. That's all any of us can hope for. I pray to be filled with the vast love of Jesus, and to love someone else for his sake.

Psalm 28:1-3. 7-9

O Lord, I call to you; my Rock, do not be deaf to my cry;
    lest, if you do not hear me,
    I become like those who go down to the Pit.
Hear the voice of my prayer when I cry out to you,
    when I lift up my hands to your holy of holies.
Do not snatch me away with the wicked or with the evildoers,
    who speak peaceably with their neighbors,
    while strife is in their hearts…
The Lord is my strength and my shield;
    my heart trusts in him, and I have been helped;
Therefore my heart dances for joy,
    and in my song will I praise him.
The Lord is the strength of his people,
    a safe refuge for his anointed.
Save your people and bless your inheritance;
    shepherd them and carry them for ever.

December Eleventh

The Prayer of the Day

Merciful God, who sent your messengers the prophets to preach repentance and prepare the way for our salvation: Give us grace to heed their warnings and forsake our sins, that we may greet with joy the coming of Jesus Christ our Redeemer; who lives and reigns with you and the Holy Spirit, one God, now and for ever. Amen.

Scripture: Zechariah 3:1-9 (NIV)

Then he showed me Joshua the high priest standing before the angel of the Lord, and Satan standing at his right side to accuse him. The Lord said to Satan, "The Lord rebuke you, Satan! The Lord, who has chosen Jerusalem, rebuke you! Is not this man a burning stick snatched from the fire?" Now Joshua was dressed in filthy clothes as he stood before the angel. The angel said to those who were standing before him, "Take off his filthy clothes." Then he said to Joshua, "See, I have taken away your sin, and I will put fine garments on you."

Then I said, "Put a clean turban on his head." So they put a clean turban on his head and clothed him, while the angel of the Lord stood by. The angel of the Lord gave this charge to Joshua: "This is what the Lord Almighty says: 'If you will walk in obedience to me and keep my requirements, then you will govern my house and have charge of my courts, and I will give you a place among these standing here.'"

"Listen, High Priest Joshua, you and your associates seated before you, who are men symbolic of things to come: I am going to bring my servant, the Branch. See, the stone I have set in front of Joshua! There are seven eyes on that one stone, and I will engrave an inscription on it," says the Lord Almighty, "and I will remove the sin of this land in a single day."

Homily: The Accuser

In this reading, the prophet Zechariah sees into God's throne room. What he witnesses is, essentially, a courtroom scene. The high priest of God, named Joshua, is on trial. The prosecuting attorney is Satan. The defense attorney and the judge seem to be the same person, the

Angel of the Lord. Satan accuses Joshua, but the Lord (or the Angel of the Lord, as they are interchangeable) rebukes Satan.

The name Joshua and the name Jesus are essentially the same (*Yehoshuah* and *Yeshuah* in Hebrew, respectively). Joshua has his rags removed and is given rule over God's house, much like Christ goes through the brutality of the crucifixion before his glorious resurrection and triumphant reign. There is the prophecy of God's "servant, the Branch" (Zechariah 3:8, NIV). Christ is called a branch from the stump of Jesse, and is the suffering servant (Isaiah 11:1 and Isaiah 53). The Lord says he will remove the guilt of the land in a single day, and so the work of Redemption is accomplished in a single day on the Cross.

I want us to consider the idea of Satan as the prosecutor. Satan is called the Accuser who "accuses our brothers and sisters before God day and night" (Revelation 12:9-11, NIV). The devil points at God's people and says "look how bad they are, you must punish them!"

Consider that for a moment. It's the devil who accuses us of our wrongdoing. Just as he did with Job (Job 1 and 2), he seeks to incite God to punish us for our sins. Contrast that with the Holy Spirit, who brings conviction to God's people. The Spirit shows us our sins so that we can repent and be forgiven. Satan, on the other hand, brings condemnation. He points out our sins so we can be tormented by guilt, shame, and self-loathing. Satan does not want us to repent and be healed, he wants us to hold tight to our sins, all the way to eternal death.

Advent is not a time to beat ourselves up about what we've done wrong. It's not a time to wallow in self-hatred. It is a time to allow the Spirit to convict us so that we can repent. But if you are tormented by guilt, shame, and self-hate, then you are not getting that from God. You are experiencing condemnation from your own mind or from the devil, or both.

As we continue to journey through Advent, let's spend time in repentance. But let's also keep focused on the Good News of the Cross. We don't need to listen to Satan. Christ came and died to set us free, not to imprison us in condemnation.

"Therefore, there is now no condemnation for those who are in Christ Jesus, because through Christ Jesus the law of the Spirit who gives life has set you free from the law of sin and death" (Romans 8:1-2, NIV).

Psalm 38:1-4, 18-22

O Lord, do not rebuke me in your anger;
> do not punish me in your wrath.

For your arrows have already pierced me,
> and your hand presses hard upon me.

There is no health in my flesh, because of your indignation;
> there is no soundness in my body, because of my sin.

For my iniquities overwhelm me;
> like a heavy burden they are too much for me to bear…

I will confess my iniquity
> and be sorry for my sin.

Those who are my enemies without cause are mighty,
> and many in number are those who wrongfully hate me.

Those who repay evil for good slander me,
> because I follow the course that is right.

O Lord, do not forsake me;
> be not far from me, O my God.

Make haste to help me,
> O Lord of my salvation.

December Twelfth

The Prayer of the Day

Merciful God, who sent your messengers the prophets to preach repentance and prepare the way for our salvation: Give us grace to heed their warnings and forsake our sins, that we may greet with joy the coming of Jesus Christ our Redeemer; who lives and reigns with you and the Holy Spirit, one God, now and for ever. Amen.

Scripture: 2 Samuel 7:8-16 (NIV)

Now then, tell my servant David, "This is what the Lord Almighty says: I took you from the pasture, from tending the flock, and appointed you ruler over my people Israel. I have been with you wherever you have gone, and I have cut off all your enemies from before you. Now I will make your name great, like the names of the greatest men on earth. And I will provide a place for my people Israel and will plant them so that they can have a home of their own and no longer be disturbed. Wicked people will not oppress them anymore, as they did at the beginning and have done ever since the time I appointed leaders over my people Israel. I will also give you rest from all your enemies."

"The Lord declares to you that the Lord himself will establish a house for you: When your days are over and you rest with your ancestors, I will raise up your offspring to succeed you, your own flesh and blood, and I will establish his kingdom. He is the one who will build a house for my Name, and I will establish the throne of his kingdom forever. I will be his father, and he will be my son. When he does wrong, I will punish him with a rod wielded by men, with floggings inflicted by human hands. But my love will never be taken away from him, as I took it away from Saul, whom I removed from before you. Your house and your kingdom will endure forever before me; your throne will be established forever."

Homily: Promises and Patience

In the scripture passage above, God promises David that the throne of his kingdom will be established forever. There will always be a son of David ruling over Israel. After David's death, his son Solomon became king. The throne then passed to David's grandson, his great-grandson, his great-great-grandson and so on.

But David's lineage did not stay faithful to David's God. Eventually, their rebellion against the Lord caused their nation to be dismantled. Their reign came to an end. With the deportation of the Jews to Babylon, there was no descendent of David on the throne. In fact, there was no throne at all. At some later points in history, the Jews ruled themselves again; but, their leaders were no longer the descendants of King David.

God did not forget his promise. When the Son of God, Jesus of Nazareth, came to our world, he was born into the bloodline of David. Born in a stable, he came to rule the cosmos. Even now, he sits eternally enthroned. Jesus, the Son of God, the Son of David, is Lord forever. None of David's other offspring could have imagined such a glorious throne.

The promise did not come the way that many would have hoped. Centuries passed in which it looked like God had forgotten Israel. Generations lived and died, and did not see the promise fulfilled.

Advent is a time when we expect the fulfillment of God's promises. God always keeps his word, but he doesn't necessarily keep it according to our vision, or our timing. He will do what he says he will do, but he may not do it in the way we wish. He will provide for us, but not necessarily give us what we want. He will save us, but may not make us feel good while he's doing it. He will help us, but his help may bring us to some difficult places.

God does not promise instant results. Advent is a time to be reminded of God's promises, but it's also a time to be patient for them. He is trustworthy to give us grace, and we must rely on that grace to stay peacefully expectant. He will fulfill his promises to his people and to his creation. But he will do it in his own time and in his own way.

Psalm 37:1-7a, 18

Do not fret yourself because of evildoers;
> do not be jealous of those who do wrong.

For they shall soon wither like the grass,
> and like the green grass fade away.

Put your trust in the Lord and do good;
> dwell in the land and feed on its riches.

Take delight in the Lord,
> and he shall give you your heart's desire.

Commit your way to the Lord and put your trust in him,
> and he will bring it to pass.

He will make your righteousness as clear as the light
> and your just dealing as the noonday.

Be still before the Lord
> and wait patiently for him…

For the power of the wicked shall be broken,
> but the Lord upholds the righteous.

December Thirteenth

The Prayer of the Day

Merciful God, who sent your messengers the prophets to preach repentance and prepare the way for our salvation: Give us grace to heed their warnings and forsake our sins, that we may greet with joy the coming of Jesus Christ our Redeemer; who lives and reigns with you and the Holy Spirit, one God, now and for ever. Amen.

Scripture: John 14:1-6 (NIV)

Jesus said to his disciples "Do not let your hearts be troubled. You believe in God; believe also in me. My Father's house has many rooms; if that were not so, would I have told you that I am going there to prepare a place for you? And if I go and prepare a place for you, I will come back and take you to be with me that you also may be where I am. You know the way to the place where I am going." Thomas said to him, "Lord, we don't know where you are going, so how can we know the way?" Jesus answered, "I am the way and the truth and the life. No one comes to the Father except through me."

Homily: Re-Ordered

I'm prone to anxiety. When I'm upset about something, I can get into a bad headspace. Instead of living in the moment, I focus on worse-case scenarios. I start to play these out in my mind until all I see is a dark future. Instead of being thankful for my many blessings, I only think of what I don't have, or what I might lose. In my stress, I get short tempered and difficult to be around.

I was in that place on a recent Saturday. I wasn't feeling in the least bit social, and I wasn't looking forward to worship on Sunday morning. The next day, I got up early to spend time with the Lord, but my mood didn't improve.

I showed up at church, I put my robe on, and I gathered with those who serve at the altar. We prayed together. As I often do, I thanked God for this time to worship, and I praised him for his Word and Sacrament. I asked him to stir up his Spirit, and to reorder our hearts and minds.

The Eucharistic Feast, our ancient pattern of worship, brought me away from the world of my feelings and thoughts. Instead of living in a universe in which my mood makes reality, the Eucharist opened my heart and mind to the Truth. That day, as I gave in to worship, God worked in me. I began to experience the love and power of Christ. As I spoke, sang, and listened, I believed again that Jesus is Lord.

I repented of my plans and anxieties. I had arrived that morning with a disordered way of thinking. I went home recognizing that Christ is enthroned, and that I am not the maker of reality.

Advent is a time for reordering. By grace, we stay focused on Christ and not on the anxieties of this world. Everything society has to offer begins to look like meaningless dust. The Lord is exalted as we look to him, and allow him to put us back in alignment with Heaven.

Psalm 31:1-5

In you, O Lord, have I taken refuge; let me never be put to shame;
    deliver me in your righteousness.
Incline your ear to me;
    make haste to deliver me.
Be my strong rock, a castle to keep me safe,
for you are my crag and my stronghold;
    for the sake of your Name, lead me and guide me.
Take me out of the net that they have secretly set for me,
    for you are my tower of strength.
Into your hands I commend my spirit,
    for you have redeemed me,
        O Lord, O God of truth.

December Fourteenth

The Prayer of the Day

Merciful God, who sent your messengers the prophets to preach repentance and prepare the way for our salvation: Give us grace to heed their warnings and forsake our sins, that we may greet with joy the coming of Jesus Christ our Redeemer; who lives and reigns with you and the Holy Spirit, one God, now and for ever. Amen.

Scripture: Isaiah 58:6-8 (NIV)

"Is not this the kind of fasting I have chosen:
to loose the chains of injustice
    and untie the cords of the yoke,
to set the oppressed free
    and break every yoke?
Is it not to share your food with the hungry
    and to provide the poor wanderer with shelter—
when you see the naked, to clothe them,
    and not to turn away from your own flesh and blood?
Then your light will break forth like the dawn,
    and your healing will quickly appear;
then your righteousness will go before you,
    and the glory of the Lord will be your rear guard.

Homily: The Advent Fast

It's Christmastime! All around us people are shopping, eating, drinking, and partying. Of course, so are we. We're celebrating, too, and why not? This is a great time of year to gather with friends and family, co-workers and fellow students. This is a season of good food and good times.

But Advent is a season of fasting. The Church has, for hundreds of years, called upon her members to treat Advent as we would Lent. In fact, the Eastern Orthodox Church refers to Advent as the "Winter Lent." We give something up, we spend more time in reflection, we take on a spiritual discipline. Does that mean we should avoid this year's office party? Maybe, maybe not. That's up to you. Let me offer this possibility.

In the Book of Isaiah, the Holy Spirit counsels us that fasting is not just about giving up food. It's also about sharing with the poor. In the secular world, the Christmas season is about buying and receiving, as well as giving to those we love. In the Church world, the Advent season is about supporting those who are in need as an act of Christian love.

This is a great time of year to make a special offering to your church. After all, the Bible tells us "So then, as we have opportunity, let us do good to everyone, and especially to those who are of the household of faith" (Galatians 6:10). It is also a good time of year to give to organizations which focus on the poor.

Most importantly, Advent opens the possibility of serving others face-to-face. Many churches and organizations offer such opportunities. You can sing carols to the elderly, hand out gifts to prisoners, or serve a meal to a homeless person. You could call someone who is lonely, send a care package to a soldier, or visit a shut-in.

Fasting isn't just about refraining from food. It's also about giving up some of your time and energy. When busy people give up our time and energy, we are showing that we trust God. God, in return, is always trustworthy.

Psalm 43:3-5

Send out your light and your truth, that they may lead me,
    and bring me to your holy hill and to your dwelling;
That I may go to the altar of God,
    to the God of my joy and gladness;
    and on the harp I will give thanks to you, O God my God.
Why are you so full of heaviness, O my soul?
    and why are you so disquieted within me?
Put your trust in God;
    for I will yet give thanks to him,
    who is the help of my countenance, and my God.

December Fifteenth

The Prayer of the Day

Stir up your power, O Lord, and with great might come among us; and, because we are sorely hindered by our sins, let your bountiful grace and mercy speedily help and deliver us; through Jesus Christ our Lord, to whom, with you and the Holy Spirit, be honor and glory, now and for ever. Amen.

Scripture: Luke 1:26-38 (NIV)

In the sixth month of Elizabeth's pregnancy, God sent the angel Gabriel to Nazareth, a town in Galilee, to a virgin pledged to be married to a man named Joseph, a descendant of David. The virgin's name was Mary. The angel went to her and said, "Greetings, you who are highly favored! The Lord is with you." Mary was greatly troubled at his words and wondered what kind of greeting this might be. But the angel said to her, "Do not be afraid, Mary; you have found favor with God. You will conceive and give birth to a son, and you are to call him Jesus. He will be great and will be called the Son of the Most High. The Lord God will give him the throne of his father David, and he will reign over Jacob's descendants forever; his kingdom will never end."

"How will this be," Mary asked the angel, "since I am a virgin?" The angel answered, "The Holy Spirit will come on you, and the power of the Most High will overshadow you. So the holy one to be born will be called the Son of God. Even Elizabeth your relative is going to have a child in her old age, and she who was said to be unable to conceive is in her sixth month. For no word from God will ever fail." "I am the Lord's servant," Mary answered. "May your word to me be fulfilled." Then the angel left her.

Homily: Blessed is She

The woman who would be called the Mother of God lived in a tiny town called Nazareth. Nazareth was part of an unimportant district known to the Romans simply as "the Circuit," a word that comes to us as "Galilee." Nazareth was "a one horse town," a rest stop between other places. It was a small, insignificant place inside a larger insignificant place.

At the time of Jesus' birth, Mary was unmarried and a virgin. Scholars agree that she was around the age of 14. Her engagement with Joseph was probably arranged by her parents. In their culture, Mary would be given over to Joseph along with some of her father's possessions (a dowry), and she would become his wife. Being a wife was a great deal like being a piece of property. Mary would be expected to have children, care for her family, and engage in the life of the village. All the years of her short existence, Mary had been training for this. There was no reason for Mary to believe her life would be any different from those of all the other women she saw every day.

Mary's life took an unexpected turn when an angel came to her. We don't know where this encounter happened, what time of day or night. We have no description of Gabriel or of Mary. We do know that this visit changed everything.

In just a few sentences in the Book of Luke, Mary showed her distress, her fear, her astonishment, and her curiosity. She was a person just like us. When an angel from God told her that she would give birth to a king who would reign forever, she focused not on the brilliant future but the practical reality staring her in the face—she'd never had sex. But she accepted the angel's mysterious explanation, and the Divine will.

In our society we have credit scores and social standing acquired through education or wealth. These things tell other people who we are and what we are worth. In Mary's society, they had honor. She lived in a tiny, close-knit community, one which was very sexually conservative. By being unmarried and pregnant, Mary had dishonored herself, her father, her family, and Joseph. She was in danger of losing everything. By becoming pregnant outside of her relationship with Joseph, there was a very real possibility that Mary would be driven out of her father's house and left to wander. Being a an unmarried pregnant, girl was a sure road to prostitution, slavery, or both.

In the midst of all that danger, Mary took an enormous risk by accepting the angel's message. She did this for her people, and for us as well. But she didn't accept this challenge in her own strength. Gabriel told Mary that she had received grace (often translated as "favor"), and it's by that grace that she was so strong.

As Christmas comes closer, I give thanks for the grace God gave to that Palestinian girl. She inspires me today to trust the Lord, and let him take care of the outcomes.

Psalm 63:1-8

O God, you are my God; eagerly I seek you;
> my soul thirsts for you, my flesh faints for you,
> > as in a barren and dry land where there is no water.

Therefore I have gazed upon you in your holy place,
> that I might behold your power and your glory.

For your loving-kindness is better than life itself;
> my lips shall give you praise.

So will I bless you as long as I live
> and lift up my hands in your Name.

My soul is content, as with marrow and fatness,
> and my mouth praises you with joyful lips,

When I remember you upon my bed,
> and meditate on you in the night watches.

For you have been my helper,
> and under the shadow of your wings I will rejoice.

My soul clings to you;
> your right hand holds me fast.

December Sixteenth

The Prayer of the Day

Stir up your power, O Lord, and with great might come among us; and, because we are sorely hindered by our sins, let your bountiful grace and mercy speedily help and deliver us; through Jesus Christ our Lord, to whom, with you and the Holy Spirit, be honor and glory, now and for ever. Amen.

Scripture: Job 2:11-13 (NIV)

When Job's three friends, Eliphaz the Temanite, Bildad the Shuhite and Zophar the Naamathite, heard about all the troubles that had come upon him, they set out from their homes and met together by agreement to go and sympathize with him and comfort him. When they saw him from a distance, they could hardly recognize him; they began to weep aloud, and they tore their robes and sprinkled dust on their heads. Then they sat on the ground with him for seven days and seven nights. No one said a word to him, because they saw how great his suffering was.

Homily: When Advent Fails

Back in the 1990s, my church decided to produce a book of Advent devotions. The lady putting it together thought I was "artsy," so she asked me to design the cover. I came up with something I thought was pretty cool. I submitted a simple black and white picture of a pregnant woman's torso in profile. This sparked all kinds of hand-wringing at the church, culminating in my pastor telling me the design was in poor taste. My design was replaced with a clip-art image of the Three Wise Men (who, by the way, have nothing to do with Advent).

Pregnancy is a wonderful image for Advent. It works on so many levels. Mary was obviously pregnant with Jesus. Time itself was, in a sense, pregnant with the Son of God (Galatians 4:4-5). Today, we might say that the cosmos is again pregnant, waiting eagerly for the children of God to come forth when Christ returns (Romans 8:19). Advent, like pregnancy, is a waiting for something marvelous.

There is a young couple whom I have known for a long time. During last year's Advent, the woman gave birth to twin sons. They were quite premature and both passed away not long after being delivered.

Their parents got to hold them for just a few precious minutes before they were gone, gone until the Resurrection at the Last Day.

According to the American Pregnancy Association's website, there are six million pregnancies every year in the United States. Of these, approximately one-third end in pregnancy loss. More than half of those are due to abortion, but 800,000 are the result of miscarriage and similar issues. Everyone knows someone who has lost a child in pregnancy, and you might well be one of them.

What happens when excitement and expectation ends in disappointment and calamity? What do you do when your Advent ends not in Christmas but in Good Friday? Expectations are not always fulfilled, hope is sometimes dashed. Sometimes this results in loss of life, as happened to my friends. Sometimes the loss is not as tragic as the death of a child, but it is no less real. Relationships end poorly, jobs fall through, dreams are not realized.

When someone is in the middle of their suffering, it is easy for an outsider to say, "God is with them." That is true, and it is the message of Advent. Christ is with the suffering, the broken, and the mourning. He knows what it means to endure horrific evil, so he is the ultimate source of comfort to the hurting.

At the same time, suffering does not always move quickly to hope. Sometimes hope is put on hold while mourning continues. For people in the middle of their pain, God may be found in the silent affection of other human beings. Christ is incarnate in the tender compassion of the friend who says, "I don't understand it either" as she bursts into tears. The Christian who can set aside her need to control, her desire to "make it better," and can sit in the awful pain of her friend becomes Jesus to that friend.

For those of you who are suffering right now, let me say a couple of things. Your pain is real and it has meaning. I encourage you to feel what you feel, to be as angry and sad and overwhelmed as you are. In the middle of your pain, please know that there is still hope for you because of Christ. I suggest that you reveal your suffering to people who can sit in it with you. I hope you will find some hope in this Advent, and in the God who has not given up on you.

Psalm 41:1-4, 10-13

Happy are they who consider the poor and needy!
>the Lord will deliver them in the time of trouble.

The Lord preserves them and keeps them alive,
so that they may be happy in the land;
>he does not hand them over to the will of their enemies.

The Lord sustains them on their sickbed
>and ministers to them in their illness.

I said, "Lord, be merciful to me;
>heal me, for I have sinned against you."...

But you, O Lord, be merciful to me and raise me up,
>and I shall repay them.

By this I know you are pleased with me,
>that my enemy does not triumph over me.

In my integrity you hold me fast,
>and shall set me before your face for ever.

Blessed be the Lord God of Israel,
>from age to age. Amen. Amen.

December Seventeenth

The Prayer of the Day

Stir up your power, O Lord, and with great might come among us; and, because we are sorely hindered by our sins, let your bountiful grace and mercy speedily help and deliver us; through Jesus Christ our Lord, to whom, with you and the Holy Spirit, be honor and glory, now and for ever. Amen.

Scripture: Colossians 1:15-20 (NIV)

The Son is the image of the invisible God, the firstborn over all creation. For in him all things were created: things in Heaven and on earth, visible and invisible, whether thrones or powers or rulers or authorities; all things have been created through him and for him. He is before all things, and in him all things hold together. And he is the head of the body, the church; he is the beginning and the firstborn from among the dead, so that in everything he might have the supremacy. For God was pleased to have all his fullness dwell in him, and through him to reconcile to himself all things, whether things on earth or things in Heaven, by making peace through his blood, shed on the cross.

Homily: Kingdom Come

St. Paul wrote, "For He rescued us from the domain of darkness, and transferred us to the kingdom of His beloved Son, in whom we have redemption, the forgiveness of sins" (Colossians 1:13, NIV). Without Christ, we live in the domain of darkness. As the Book of Colossians continues, we see that darkness rules us on many levels. We live under the dominion of false gods and the natural forces of the world. We live under the weight of philosophies and religion. We constantly have to prove ourselves to our rulers and authority figures.

Christ didn't destroy these rulers. Instead, he came to rescue us from their power. He transferred us out of their authority and into the domain of his glorious kingdom. Do governments, rules, and religions exist? Yes, of course. Are they sometimes good and helpful? Certainly. Do they control our destinies? No, not at all.

This is the truth of Advent: the King is coming. He is not one of many rulers; rather, he is the sole King, the only legitimate ruler. In his great power, he comes among us. He rescues us from our sin. He even rescues us from our own self-righteousness.

Are we then free to act however we please? No. We are called to do right, to live good and godly lives. But how we act is not the foundation of who we are. Our identity is not found in good or bad behavior. It's found in the triumph of Jesus.

When I do good, I belong to Jesus. When I sin, I belong to Jesus. When I disappoint someone, I still belong to Jesus. His authority is absolute. I am no longer judged by the standards of this world, but on the finished work of Christ.

Psalm 47

Clap your hands, all you peoples;
    shout to God with a cry of joy.
For the Lord Most High is to be feared;
    he is the great King over all the earth.
He subdues the peoples under us,
    and the nations under our feet.
He chooses our inheritance for us,
    the pride of Jacob whom he loves.
God has gone up with a shout,
    the Lord with the sound of the ram's-horn.
Sing praises to God, sing praises;
    sing praises to our King, sing praises.
For God is King of all the earth;
    sing praises with all your skill.
God reigns over the nations;
    God sits upon his holy throne.
The nobles of the peoples have gathered together
    with the people of the God of Abraham.
The rulers of the earth belong to God,
    and he is highly exalted.

December Eighteenth

The Prayer of the Day

Stir up your power, O Lord, and with great might come among us; and, because we are sorely hindered by our sins, let your bountiful grace and mercy speedily help and deliver us; through Jesus Christ our Lord, to whom, with you and the Holy Spirit, be honor and glory, now and for ever. Amen.

Scripture: Romans 5:6-8 (NIV)

You see, at just the right time, when we were still powerless, Christ died for the ungodly. Very rarely will anyone die for a righteous person, though for a good person someone might possibly dare to die. But God demonstrates his own love for us in this: While we were still sinners, Christ died for us.

Homily: There is no Santa Claus

When I was a child, my family had an interesting way of preparing for Christmas. We had a twenty-five day Advent calendar on the refrigerator. Each day, my parents would decide if my sister and I had been "naughty" or "nice." If we had been nice, we were allowed to put a star on our calendar. Naughty days meant no stars. I had the silver stars, my sister the gold. The number of stars was supposed to have some kind of effect on the number of presents Santa would give us on Christmas Day. If we were good enough, the mysterious, eternal man from far away would reward us.

Some adults still believe in Santa Claus, but now they call him "God."

I think there are good arguments for telling children about Santa Claus, and I have no interest in condemning people who participate in that fun tradition. That said, my wife and I didn't tell our kids about Santa when they were little. An old man who lives far away, watching everyone on earth, keeping track of good and bad deeds, and then rewarding accordingly? That sounds a lot like the god of false religion.

The message of the Gospel is that our Father's love for us is greater than our behavior. His love precedes our actions. He loved us before we existed. He didn't wait for us to "get right" before saving us.

While we were sitting in our sin, while we were living in open rebellion, Jesus came for us and died for us. Our salvation is from his grace, and is in no way related to our good works. Good works are vital to meaningful lives. But, they are the result of our Father's love, not the cause. We can't earn God's love because his love is unchanging.

Tell your kids and grandkids about Santa Claus, or don't. Up to you. Just don't believe in Santa Claus yourself. There is no distant, omniscient being who accepts or rejects you based on your behavior. There is a God who is closer to you than your breath, more compassionate than you know, and more willing to bless you than you are willing to ask. He desires that you do good, but his love for you will never be based on the good or bad you've done. His love is based on the good that he has done.

Psalm 119:57-64

You only are my portion, O Lord;
    I have promised to keep your words.
I entreat you with all my heart,
    be merciful to me according to your promise.
I have considered my ways
    and turned my feet toward your decrees.
I hasten and do not tarry
    to keep your commandments.
Though the cords of the wicked entangle me,
    I do not forget your law.
At midnight I will rise to give you thanks,
    because of your righteous judgments.
I am a companion of all who fear you;
    and of those who keep your commandments.
The earth, O Lord, is full of your love;
    instruct me in your statutes.

December Nineteenth

The Prayer of the Day

Purify our conscience, Almighty God, by your daily visitation, that your Son Jesus Christ, at his coming, may find in us a mansion prepared for himself; who lives and reigns with you, in the unity of the Holy Spirit, one God, now and for ever. Amen.

Scripture: Matthew 1:18-25 (NIV)

This is how the birth of Jesus the Messiah came about: His mother Mary was pledged to be married to Joseph, but before they came together, she was found to be pregnant through the Holy Spirit. Because Joseph her husband was faithful to the law, and yet did not want to expose her to public disgrace, he had in mind to divorce her quietly.

But after he had considered this, an angel of the Lord appeared to him in a dream and said, "Joseph son of David, do not be afraid to take Mary home as your wife, because what is conceived in her is from the Holy Spirit. She will give birth to a son, and you are to give him the name Jesus, because he will save his people from their sins."

All this took place to fulfill what the Lord had said through the prophet: "The virgin will conceive and give birth to a son, and they will call him Immanuel" (which means "God with us"). When Joseph woke up, he did what the angel of the Lord had commanded him and took Mary home as his wife. But he did not consummate their marriage until she gave birth to a son. And he gave him the name Jesus.

Homily: Blessed is He

We know very little about Jesus' adopted father. He was probably a woodworker, about 20 years old. His family came from Judea, but he lived in a tiny town in Galilee. That's all the information we have.

By the time Joseph appears in the Book of Matthew, Mary was already pregnant. She had been away from Nazareth for about three months, staying with her cousin. By the time she came back, it was obvious that she was going to have a baby. It's quite possible Mary didn't tell Joseph that she was pregnant or how it happened. He may have found out the same way everyone else had: by looking at her.

Regardless of how he discovered the pregnancy, Joseph showed remarkable compassion and restraint. In those days an engagement was a legal contract. Joseph could have claimed that his "property" had been damaged. He could have publicly humiliated Mary and her family. Instead, the New Testament tells us that he "did not want to expose her to public disgrace" (Matthew 1:19, NIV).

It was at this moment that Joseph had a dream. God revealed that Mary's pregnancy was from the Holy Spirit. The Bible then says that Joseph took Mary home with him, but they did not have sexual relations until after she had given birth (Matthew 1:24-25).

Joseph and Mary moved in together while she was pregnant. When this happened, they were assumed to be married. No ceremony is mentioned, just the fact of cohabitation. The other villagers thought that the baby was his, or at least he would raise it has his own. In their eyes Joseph was either immoral (for sleeping with the girl before they were married) or a fool (for marrying a "damaged" girl).

Joseph could have rejected God's plan. He could have said that he was entitled to a normal life, a life of honor and respect. Instead, he suffered rejection for God's sake. Entitlement is the belief that you deserve things to go your way. God or the Universe owes you something. When you don't get what you want, you become angry and bitter. Entitlement is one of the most disastrous of spiritual sicknesses.

Joseph rejected entitlement. When it seemed as if Mary had broken her contract, he decided to be merciful. When God told him he would have to raise a son who was not his, he took Mary and the boy into his home. When Joseph was forced to go to Bethlehem and then flee to Egypt, he moved forward in God's plan with no recorded complaint. He is a man who did not get what he wanted, and yet was faithful to the Lord and to his family. He is a model for us today.

May God give us the grace to lay down our entitlements, like Joseph did. May God give that grace to all his Church in this Advent season.

Psalm 8

O Lord our Governor,
>how exalted is your Name in all the world!

Out of the mouths of infants and children
>your majesty is praised above the Heavens.

You have set up a stronghold against your adversaries,
>to quell the enemy and the avenger.

When I consider your Heavens, the work of your fingers,
>the moon and the stars you have set in their courses,

What is man that you should be mindful of him?
>the son of man that you should seek him out?

You have made him but little lower than the angels;
>you adorn him with glory and honor;

You give him mastery over the works of your hands;
>you put all things under his feet:

All sheep and oxen,
>even the wild beasts of the field,

The birds of the air, the fish of the sea,
>and whatsoever walks in the paths of the sea.

O Lord our Governor,
>how exalted is your Name in all the world!

December Twentieth

The Prayer of the Day

Stir up your power, O Lord, and with great might come among us; and, because we are sorely hindered by our sins, let your bountiful grace and mercy speedily help and deliver us; through Jesus Christ our Lord, to whom, with you and the Holy Spirit, be honor and glory, now and for ever. Amen.

Scripture: Matthew 16:1-4 (NIV)

The Pharisees and Sadducees came to Jesus and tested him by asking him to show them a sign from Heaven. He replied, "When evening comes, you say, 'It will be fair weather, for the sky is red,' and in the morning, 'Today it will be stormy, for the sky is red and overcast.' You know how to interpret the appearance of the sky, but you cannot interpret the signs of the times. A wicked and adulterous generation looks for a sign, but none will be given it except the sign of Jonah." Jesus then left them and went away.

Homily: The Sign of Jonah

One night in December, I went for a walk. I hesitated to go out because it was so cold. But I needed the exercise, so I put on my heaviest coat, my gloves, and my ski mask. Out I went.

The next night, just 24 hours later, I went out for a run. This time I wore a t-shirt. In the short time from one night to the next, the temperature had changed dramatically. from 23° F to 54°.

Weather changes, sometimes slowly, sometimes rapidly. I find the same is true of my mood. I can be going along feeling great, and then the smallest thing can irk me. Or I may be feeling sad about something, but then my wife or one of my daughters says something kind and I'm out of it. Sometimes I can see a shift coming, but other times it takes me by surprise.

The spiritual life can be like this. I can go from praising God for this faithfulness to doubting whether or not he is even real. Sometimes, this change can take place quickly. A bill will come in, or an unwelcome phone call, or a flip comment from a friend. These affect not only my emotions, but also my trust in God. I wish I was constant, like a rock. But I'm not.

What I sometimes want is a sign from God that he's paying attention, that he hasn't forgotten me. I think, "If only God would reveal himself to me, then I would feel OK." It's as if I want God to prove that he's real, and I want that proof again and again.

The religious leaders of Jesus' day were looking to God for a sign. They were supposedly looking for the Messiah, but he was standing right in front of them. I can be like that, testing God because I'm angry. Other times, though, I'm honestly searching. In either case, I'm given the Sign of Jonah.

That phrase, "The Sign of Jonah," is a reference to an event in the Old Testament. Jonah the prophet was swallowed up by a great fish. He lived in the belly of that fish for three days, and then was spit back up. Jonah was in the heart of darkness until he suddenly returned. Similarly, Christ was swallowed up by death for three days. He went straight into the unknown, but then he returned. The greatest sign God has ever given us is the Resurrection of Jesus Christ.

Jesus has already won the victory. He has already conquered my greatest enemies: Sin, Death, Hell, and the Devil. While I may or may not be feeling very well at this moment, he is present. He has given me a sign, one that reminds me that he will never leave me or forsake me. That sign is his Cross and Resurrection. I don't need a better one. Rather than looking for a good event or a happy feeling, I can find comfort in the finished work of Christ.

Psalm 40:1-5

I waited patiently upon the Lord;
    he stooped to me and heard my cry.
He lifted me out of the desolate pit, out of the mire and clay;
    he set my feet upon a high cliff and made my footing sure.
He put a new song in my mouth, a song of praise to our God;
    many shall see, and stand in awe,
    and put their trust in the Lord.
Happy are they who trust in the Lord!
    they do not resort to evil spirits or turn to false gods.
Great things are they that you have done, O Lord my God!
    how great your wonders and your plans for us!

December Twenty-first

The Prayer of the Day

Stir up your power, O Lord, and with great might come among us; and, because we are sorely hindered by our sins, let your bountiful grace and mercy speedily help and deliver us; through Jesus Christ our Lord, to whom, with you and the Holy Spirit, be honor and glory, now and for ever. Amen.

Scripture: Revelation 5:9-14 (NIV)

And they sang a new song, saying:
"You are worthy to take the scroll
   and to open its seals,
because you were slain,
   and with your blood you purchased for God
   persons from every tribe and language and people and nation.
You have made them to be a kingdom and priests to serve our God,
   and they will reign on the earth."
Then I looked and heard the voice of many angels, numbering thousands upon thousands, and ten thousand times ten thousand. They encircled the throne and the living creatures and the elders. In a loud voice they were saying:
"Worthy is the Lamb, who was slain,
   to receive power and wealth and wisdom and strength
   and honor and glory and praise!"
Then I heard every creature in Heaven and on earth and under the earth and on the sea, and all that is in them, saying:
"To him who sits on the throne and to the Lamb
   be praise and honor and glory and power, for ever and ever!"
The four living creatures said, "Amen," and the elders fell down and worshiped.

Homily: Can I Get an Amen?

I'm a huge fan of Handel's Messiah. I'm especially fond of the tenor solos, and the Isaiah texts. The Hallelujah Chorus is, of course, a highlight. But, of the entire piece, my favorite part is the final chorus, "Worthy is the Lamb." It's taken from Revelation, chapter five, and says:

> Worthy is the Lamb that was slain to receive power, and riches, and wisdom, and strength, and honour, and glory, and blessing. Blessing, and honour, glory and power, be unto Him that sitteth upon the throne, and unto the Lamb, for ever and ever. Amen.

It probably took you a few seconds to read those words. It takes a great deal longer to sing them. The Amens by themselves go on for quite some time. These Amens minister to my soul. Musically they are transcendent, but that is not why I love them so much. I love them because they remind me that Heaven itself says "Amen."

The Amen is the final ending to all that is taking place on earth, and that word belongs to God alone. Amen means that everything will come to a conclusion, that all that has gone before will be summed up. The eternal purpose of my life will be made known, and that purpose will rest entirely in the grace of Christ.

Right now, I need that Amen. I need a conclusion to my concerns, my worries, and my questions. I need God to have the final word on all that I am going through, both the good and the bad. I need my mind and heart to be reordered. I want to look into the Heavenly throne room, I want to see the angels of God giving him glory and honor. I want to get my eyes off of myself and on to Christ. I want to join with the four living creatures and sing a great 'AMEN' to those praises.

May God grant you an Advent in which you catch a glimpse of that Amen. May you trust that this Amen will come. Our God reigns now, and he will reign forever and ever. Amen.

Psalm 138

I will give thanks to you, O Lord, with my whole heart;
> before the gods I will sing your praise.
I will bow down toward your holy temple and praise your Name,
> because of your love and faithfulness;
For you have glorified your Name
> and your word above all things.
When I called, you answered me;
> you increased my strength within me.
All the kings of the earth will praise you, O Lord,
> when they have heard the words of your mouth.
They will sing of the ways of the Lord,
> that great is the glory of the Lord.
Though the Lord be high, he cares for the lowly;
> he perceives the haughty from afar.
Though I walk in the midst of trouble, you keep me safe;
> you stretch forth your hand against the fury of my enemies;
> your right hand shall save me.
The Lord will make good his purpose for me;
> O Lord, your love endures for ever;
> do not abandon the works of your hands.

December Twenty-second

The Prayer of the Day

Stir up your power, O Lord, and with great might come among us; and, because we are sorely hindered by our sins, let your bountiful grace and mercy speedily help and deliver us; through Jesus Christ our Lord, to whom, with you and the Holy Spirit, be honor and glory, now and for ever. Amen.

Scripture: Luke 2:1-7 (NIV)

In those days Caesar Augustus issued a decree that a census should be taken of the entire Roman world. (This was the first census that took place while Quirinius was governor of Syria.) And everyone went to their own town to register. So Joseph also went up from the town of Nazareth in Galilee to Judea, to Bethlehem the town of David, because he belonged to the house and line of David. He went there to register with Mary, who was pledged to be married to him and was expecting a child. While they were there, the time came for the baby to be born, and she gave birth to her firstborn, a son. She wrapped him in cloths and placed him in a manger, because there was no guest room available for them.

Homily: No Room in the House

In the commonly told Christmas story, Joseph and Mary journeyed to a crowded Bethlehem. Men and women were there from all over the Jewish world. These crowds had traveled, like them, to register for the Roman census. Because of the numbers of visitors in town, there was no room for the couple in the local hotels. Joseph went from door to door, searching valiantly for a place for his betrothed to give birth. Fortunately, a kindly innkeeper told them they could sleep with his animals. So he either placed them in a barn or a cave, depending on the version of the story. In that barn, the Son of God was born.

It's truly a lovely story, but there is a small problem—it isn't exactly what the Bible says. Luke's Gospel tells us, "While they were there, the time came for the baby to be born, and she gave birth to her firstborn, a son. She wrapped him in cloths and placed him in a manger, because there was no guest room available for them." (Luke 2:6-7, NIV)

Some translations say "there was no room in the inn." Those translations are inaccurate. In Greek, the original language of the New Testament, there is a perfectly good word for "inn." That word is not found in this story. Rather, the writer says there was no "living space" available for them. This phrase, "living space" refers to a room in a house which has been designated for humans. In this culture, people kept both animals and people in the same house. After all, animals were valuable. To keep them out in a separate barn or a cave would have been both foolish and impractical, especially in a town. People had a room or two in their homes for their families, and then a room for the animals. Often this room was a step or two down from the rest of the dwelling.

Joseph and Mary didn't spend the night in a barn. They spent the night in something more like a garage, a really smelly one. Moreover, the garage wasn't attached to a hotel. It most likely belonged to Joseph's relatives.

Imagine this scene. Joseph is a distant relative from out in the sticks. He brings his young, pregnant fiancé to the big city. No one knows who the baby's father is, though these two blame the mess on God. Joseph is poor, has a funny accent, and lives in an area known for mixed races and pagan worship. His cousins in Bethlehem share little more than ancestry. They are of a higher and more pure class than these two bumpkins. They don't want to have anything to do with Joseph and his girlfriend.

However, because of their honor, the family can't let Joseph and Mary sleep in the street. That just wouldn't do, not in a culture so invested in hospitality. At the same time, they can't have these people in their house. They certainly don't want a quasi-bastard born under their roof. What to do?

They put the man and his girlfriend in the garage, with the animals. Yes, they offered hospitality. But they also made sure that Joseph and Mary knew their place. The visitors were in no position to refuse.

This story won't be shown at our church Christmas pageant. No one sings songs about Joseph's family rejecting him. And this is just one possibility, of course. The truth might be that the family home was just too crowded, that there was literally nowhere else but with the animals. No one knows for sure.

Christ was always an outsider. Though he is the Son of God and the King of the Universe, he was born to a lowly couple. As John's Gospel says "he came to that which was his own, but his own people did not receive him" (John 1:11, NIV). He was such an outcast that he wasn't even born in a room fit for humans. Rather, he was born among animals and laid in a feeding trough.

During this Advent season, you may feel cast out. Perhaps you feel like the black sheep of your family. You feel rejected, like they would rather have you sleep in the garage. Or perhaps you are the one looking down your nose at your relatives. You just can't bear the thought of those people coming into your home. In either case, it's important to remember that the One we are expecting comes to us through the lowest of places. He knows what it means to be rejected, and he implores us to receive the lowly in his Name.

Psalm 69:31-38

As for me, I am afflicted and in pain;
    your help, O God, will lift me up on high.
I will praise the Name of God in song;
    I will proclaim his greatness with thanksgiving.
This will please the Lord more than an offering of oxen,
    more than bullocks with horns and hoofs.
The afflicted shall see and be glad;
    you who seek God, your heart shall live.
For the Lord listens to the needy,
    and his prisoners he does not despise.
Let the Heavens and the earth praise him,
    the seas and all that moves in them;
For God will save Zion and rebuild the cities of Judah;
    they shall live there and have it in possession.
The children of his servants will inherit it,
    and those who love his Name will dwell therein.

December Twenty-third

The Prayer of the Day

Purify our conscience, Almighty God, by your daily visitation, that your Son Jesus Christ, at his coming, may find in us a mansion prepared for himself; who lives and reigns with you, in the unity of the Holy Spirit, one God, now and for ever. Amen.

Scripture: Matthew 24:30-35 (NIV)

"Then will appear the sign of the Son of Man in Heaven. And then all the peoples of the earth will mourn when they see the Son of Man coming on the clouds of Heaven, with power and great glory. And he will send his angels with a loud trumpet call, and they will gather his elect from the four winds, from one end of the Heavens to the other."

"Now learn this lesson from the fig tree: As soon as its twigs get tender and its leaves come out, you know that summer is near. Even so, when you see all these things, you know that it is near, right at the door. Truly I tell you, this generation will certainly not pass away until all these things have happened. Heaven and earth will pass away, but my words will never pass away."

Homily: Steward and King

Perhaps you've read the Lord of the Rings trilogy, or have seen the movies. I'm a huge fan. Recently, while watching the Fellowship of the Ring, I was struck by the character named Boromir. As you may recall, Boromir is from a country called Gondor. Many years before, the King of Gondor left his people and did not return. Since then, the kingdom had been governed by a succession of men whose title was "The Steward of Gondor." The Steward's job was to keep the throne open for the eventual return of the true King.

The Steward is a lot like us. Our King, through his Ascension, has gone away. He tells us that he is coming again. In the meantime, we are left to watch after the Kingdom on his behalf. Of course, this comparison is incomplete. We are not alone. Christ is present with us, we have the Holy Spirit, and he rules his Kingdom. But the parallel is still there.

In the Lord of the Rings, some of the people of Gondor have given up on waiting. The current Steward of Gondor acts as if he is the King. Boromir is the eldest son of the Steward, so he will become Steward when his father dies. When Boromir meets a man named Aragorn, he learns that Aragorn may be the rightful heir and true King of Gondor. This does not make Boromir happy. In the film version, he practically spits out the words, "Gondor has no king; Gondor needs no king."

How many times have we felt that way? When things are going well, it's easy for us to think that we don't need a King, we don't need a God. When things are going poorly, when we are fed up, we might also say that we don't need him. Sometimes we pay lip service to wanting a King, but our lives and actions show that we would rather not have one. We would rather rule ourselves.

As the Lord of the Rings story progresses, Boromir gets to know Aragorn. He finds someone who is strong yet compassionate, wise yet humble, a leader who is a servant. The time comes when Boromir is gravely injured and can no longer continue his journey with Aragorn. Boromir looks up at him and says, "I would have followed you, my brother…my captain…my king."

Boromir didn't want a king because he had never known a good one. He had only known self-serving rulers. But as he got to know Aragorn, he came to respect him, trust him, and even love him. Perhaps we are like Boromir. Perhaps we would rather take care of ourselves because we don't know a better alternative.

But what if there is a better alternative? What if Jesus Christ is a good, loving, and merciful King? What if Jesus is as good as they say he is? If he is, then he's a King worth following, even a King worth turning our lives over to.

Psalm 113

Hallelujah!
Give praise, you servants of the Lord;
    praise the Name of the Lord.
Let the Name of the Lord be blessed,
    from this time forth for evermore.
From the rising of the sun to its going down
    let the Name of the Lord be praised.
The Lord is high above all nations,
    and his glory above the Heavens.
Who is like the Lord our God, who sits enthroned on high
    but stoops to behold the Heavens and the earth?
He takes up the weak out of the dust
    and lifts up the poor from the ashes.
He sets them with the princes,
    with the princes of his people.
He makes the woman of a childless house
    to be a joyful mother of children.

December Twenty-fourth

The Prayer of the Day

O God, you have caused this holy night to shine with the brightness of the true Light: Grant that we, who have known the mystery of that Light on earth, may also enjoy him perfectly in Heaven; where with you and the Holy Spirit he lives and reigns, one God, in glory everlasting. Amen.

Scripture: John 1:1-5, 9-14 (NIV)

In the beginning was the Word, and the Word was with God, and the Word was God. He was with God in the beginning. Through him all things were made; without him nothing was made that has been made. In him was life, and that life was the light of all mankind. The light shines in the darkness, and the darkness has not overcome it.

The true light that gives light to everyone was coming into the world. He was in the world, and though the world was made through him, the world did not recognize him. He came to that which was his own, but his own did not receive him. Yet to all who did receive him, to those who believed in his name, he gave the right to become children of God—children born not of natural descent, nor of human decision or a husband's will, but born of God. The Word became flesh and made his dwelling among us. We have seen his glory, the glory of the one and only Son, who came from the Father, full of grace and truth.

Homily: Christmas Eve

Even as a child, I preferred Christmas Eve over Christmas Day. Anticipation is almost always better than the thing anticipated. The wrapped present under the tree is filled with wonder, far more than the unwrapped thing that will be stuffed in a drawer by New Year's Day.

A wrapped present is a symbol of hope. An unwrapped present is an object that was manufactured at a factory in China. A wrapped present is mystery, an unwrapped present is utility. A wrapped present is joy while an unwrapped present is a mere commodity.

Now imagine if the gift really was better than the expectation. That would be miraculous. You think you are in for another pair of socks, but then something extraordinary happens. You get a gift that far exceeds what you could have hoped for.

Paradise is like that. It's something we hope for, but it far surpasses the hope we have. In his Revelation, St. John uses many images for Heaven. He talks about gates made from pearl and streets paved with gold. He uses these images to say that everything in Heaven is beautiful and precious. The reality of Heaven will be even greater than the images he uses. Gold and pearls will pale in comparison to the reality we will experience.

When Christ came as a baby, the angels sang his praises to a limited number of shepherds. When Christ returns, everything in Heaven and on earth will sing his praise. No one will need to point the way to him or seek him out. No one will miss that awesome event, as most of the world missed his birth. He will be as obvious as the Sun on a cloudless day, as loud as thunder that has come too close.

How we will greet Christ depends in part on how we live in the ongoing Advent season of our daily lives. If we are not watching, not waiting, then I expect we are in for a rude awakening. If we are waiting with fear, trying to make sure we are doing enough to earn his favor, I expect we will be in for a shock when we see the Last being made First. If we are waiting with hope, as a child longing for a gift wrapped in paper and bows, I believe that the joy we find will far exceed our expectations.

Psalm 89:19-29

You spoke once in a vision
and said to your faithful people:
  "I have set the crown upon a warrior
    and have exalted one chosen out of the people.
I have found David my servant;
  with my holy oil have I anointed him.
My hand will hold him fast
  and my arm will make him strong.
No enemy shall deceive him,
  nor any wicked man bring him down.
I will crush his foes before him
  and strike down those who hate him.
My faithfulness and love shall be with him,
  and he shall be victorious through my Name.
I shall make his dominion extend
  from the Great Sea to the River.
He will say to me, 'You are my Father,
  my God, and the rock of my salvation.'
I will make him my firstborn
  and higher than the kings of the earth.
I will keep my love for him for ever,
  and my covenant will stand firm for him.
I will establish his line for ever
  and his throne as the days of Heaven."

December Twenty-fifth

The Prayer of the Day

O God, you make us glad by the yearly festival of the birth of your only Son Jesus Christ: Grant that we, who joyfully receive him as our Redeemer, may with sure confidence behold him when he comes to be our Judge; who lives and reigns with you and the Holy Spirit, one God, now and for ever. Amen.

Scripture: Luke 2:8-20 (NIV)

And there were shepherds living out in the fields nearby, keeping watch over their flocks at night. An angel of the Lord appeared to them, and the glory of the Lord shone around them, and they were terrified. But the angel said to them, "Do not be afraid. I bring you good news that will cause great joy for all the people. Today in the town of David a Savior has been born to you; he is the Messiah, the Lord. This will be a sign to you: You will find a baby wrapped in cloths and lying in a manger."

Suddenly a great company of the Heavenly host appeared with the angel, praising God and saying,
>"Glory to God in the highest Heaven,
> and on earth peace to those on whom his favor rests."

When the angels had left them and gone into Heaven, the shepherds said to one another, "Let's go to Bethlehem and see this thing that has happened, which the Lord has told us about."

So they hurried off and found Mary and Joseph, and the baby, who was lying in the manger. When they had seen him, they spread the word concerning what had been told them about this child, and all who heard it were amazed at what the shepherds said to them. But Mary treasured up all these things and pondered them in her heart. The shepherds returned, glorifying and praising God for all the things they had heard and seen, which were just as they had been told.

Homily: Emmanuel

Today is a day of celebration, the first day of the twelve-day Christmas season. You've been preparing for twenty-five days for this moment. Enjoy yourself. Spend time with people you love. If you're alone, do something special for yourself.

If your church offers a Christmas Day service, please attend. While Christmas is often thought of as a family holiday, it is first and foremost a holy day of the Church. If your congregation does not have a Christmas Day service, find a church that does. These services are not well-attended, of course. Most people have other things going on. But worship is the very best thing to do on the Day of the Incarnation.

Whatever you do today, remember that Jesus is with you. In his Incarnation, he became Emmanuel, "God with us." Through his Resurrection and Ascension, he is with us still. No matter what's happening in your life today—whether you're alone in an empty apartment, enjoying a house filled with family, at the beach, or in a hospital bed—God has not left you orphaned. He is with you. And he will come to you again and again.

Psalm 110:1-5

The Lord said to my Lord, "Sit at my right hand,
    until I make your enemies your footstool."
The Lord will send the scepter of your power out of Zion,
    saying, "Rule over your enemies round about you.
Princely state has been yours from the day of your birth;
    in the beauty of holiness have I begotten you,
    like dew from the womb of the morning."
The Lord has sworn and he will not recant:
    "You are a priest for ever after the order of Melchizedek."
The Lord who is at your right hand
    will smite kings in the day of his wrath;
    he will rule over the nations.

About the Author

The Reverend Thomas McKenzie lives in Nashville with his amazing wife and two terrific daughters. He's the author of the *The Anglican Way: A Guidebook,* which will be released in the spring of 2014.

He was born and raised near Amarillo, Texas. His Bachelor's degree is from the University of Texas at Austin, and his Master's Degree in Divinity is from Trinity School for Ministry in Ambridge, Pennsylvania.

Thomas is a priest of the Anglican Church in North America and the Anglican Diocese of Pittsburgh. He's the founding pastor of Church of the Redeemer in Nashville, Tennessee. He's an oblate of the Monastery of Christ in the Desert in Abiquiu, New Mexico.

Thomas' website is ThomasMcKenzie.com. He writes for RabbitRoom.com and AnglicanPastor.com, podcasts at RedeemerCast.net, and reviews movies at OneMinuteReview.com. He occasionally speaks at retreats, conferences, and other events. Contact him for booking information through his website, on Twitter @thomasmckenzie, or e-mail Thomas@ThomasMcKenzie.com.

Made in the USA
San Bernardino, CA
30 November 2017